History of America
The Rise to World Power
1929 to 1948

Sally Senzell Isaacs

Heinemann

First published in Great Britain by Heinemann Library,
Halley Court, Jordan Hill, Oxford OX2 8EJ,
a division of Reed Educational and Professional Publishing Ltd.
Heinemann is a registered trademark of Reed Educational & Professional
Publishing Limited.

OXFORD MELBOURNE AUCKLAND
JOHANNESBURG BLANTYRE GABORONE
IBADAN PORTSMOUTH NH (USA) CHICAGO

© Bender Richardson White 1999
© Illustrations: Bender Richardson White 1999
The moral right of the proprietor has been asserted.

HISTORY OF AMERICA: THE RISE TO WORLD POWER
was produced for Heinemann Library by Bender Richardson White.

Editor: Lionel Bender
Designer: Ben White
Assistant Editor: Michael March
Picture Researcher: Pembroke Herbert and Nancy Carter
Media Conversion and Typesetting: MW Graphics
Production Controller: Kim Richardson

03 02 01 00
10 9 8 7 6 5 4 3 2 1

Printed in Hong Kong

British Library Cataloguing-in-Publication Data.
Isaacs, Sally Senzell
  The Rise to World Power, 1929–48. – (History of America)
  1. United States - History - 1901–1953 - Juvenile literature
  I. Title.
  973.9'1

ISBN 0431 05631 5 (Hb)   ISBN 0431 05637 4 (Pb)

Acknowledgements
The producers of this book would like to thank the following for permission to
reproduce photographs:
Picture Research Consultants, Mass: pages 11t (Franklin D. Roosevelt Library,
Hyde Park, New York), 11b (University of Washington Library, Seattle,
Washington), 12 (Franklin D. Roosevelt Library, Hyde Park, New York/ACME), 13
(Franklin D. Roosevelt Library, Hyde Park, New York), 16 (PhotoAssist,
Inc./National Archives), 17, 20b (Franklin D. Roosevelt Library, Hyde Park, New
York/World Wide), 22, 26 (National Archives), 28 (Franklin D. Roosevelt Library,
Hyde Park, New York), 30, 32 (US Army Photograph/National Archives), 35c
(Robert F. Sargent/Library of Congress), 36 (National Archives: Suitland, courtesy
of the United States Holocaust Memorial Museum), 37 (National Archives). Peter
Newark's American Pictures: pages 7t, 7b, 8, 9, 15t, 15b, 18, 19, 20t, 23, 27,
31, 40, 41. Peter Newark's Military Pictures: 29, 33, 35t, 35b, 39t, 39b.
AKG Photo London: 25 (E. Gnilka).

Illustrations by: John James on pages 6/7, 12/13, 14/15, 16/17, 24/25,
26/27, 28/29, 32/33, 36/37 ; Gerald Wood on pages 8/9, 10/11, 22/23,
30/31, 38/39; James Field on pages 18/19, 34/35, 40/41.
All maps by Stefan Chabluk.
Cover design and make-up by Pelican Graphics. Artwork by John James.
Photos: all from Peter Newark's American or Military Pictures.

Special thanks to Mike Carpenter, Scott Westerfield and Tristan Boyer at
Heinemann Library for editorial and design guidance and direction.

For more information about Heinemann Library books, or to order, please phone
01865 888066, or send a fax to 01865 314091. You can visit our web site at
www.heinemann.co.uk

Any words appearing in the text in **bold, like this**, are
explained in the Glossary.

Major quotations used in this book come from the
following sources. Some of the quotations have been
abridged for clarity.
Page 14: Letter from Dust Bowl from *Down and Out in the
Great Depression*, edited by Robert S. McElvaine. Chapel
Hill: University of North Carolina Press,1983, page 75.
Page 16: Roosevelt speech in Atlanta on 29 November
1935, from *Public Papers and Addresses of Franklin D.
Roosevelt (1935)*, edited by Samuel I. Rosenman. New
York: Harper & Bros, 1950, page 474.
Pages 24: Roosevelt State of the Union speech, 6 January
1941.
Page 26: Churchill's conversation with FDR from *The
Second World War* by Winston Churchill and the Editors of
Life. New York: Golden Press, 1960, page 153.
Page 26: Roosevelt's address to Congress on 8
December 1941.
Page 27: FDR speaking to Grace Tully from Tully's account
in *Eyewitness to America*, edited by David Colbert. New
York: Pantheon Books, 1997, page 405.
Page 34: Andy Rooney's quote from *My War* by Andy
Rooney. New York: Times Books/Random House, Inc.,
1995, page 151.
Page 38: FDR's proposed speech from *Roosevelt: The
Soldier of Freedom* by James MacGregor Burns. New
York: Smithmark Publishers, Inc., 1970, page 597.

The Consultants
Special thanks to Diane Smolinski, Nancy Cope
and Christopher Gibb for their help in the
preparation of this book.

CONTENTS

History of America is a series of nine books arranged chronologically, meaning that events are described in the order in which they happened. However, each book focuses on an important person in American history, so the timespans of the titles overlap. In each book, most articles deal with a particular event or part of American history. Others deal with aspects of everyday life, such as trade, houses, clothing and farming. These general articles cover longer periods of time. The little illustrations at the top left of each article are a symbol of the times. They are identified on page 3.

▼ About the map

This map shows the United States today. It shows the boundaries and names of all the states. Refer to this map, or to the one on pages 42–43, to locate places talked about in this book.

About this book

This book is about America from 1929 to 1948. The term America means 'the United States of America' (also called the US). The United States suffered severe economic depressions five times in its history. This book covers the worst depression in our history: the Great Depression that began in 1929. World War II (WWII) was a long, complicated struggle between many nations of the world. This book focuses on America's role in the war and how it affected the lives of US citizens. Words in **bold** are described in more detail in the Glossary on page 46.

INTRODUCTION

The years between 1929 and 1948 were very good and very bad. The 1920s had been a happy and prosperous time for the country. Cars, radios and motion pictures helped Americans enjoy more experiences. Factories made more goods than ever before, and jobs were more plentiful. By the end of 1929, the country had plunged into the worst economic conditions in history. The economic crisis affected not only the United States, but also Britain and many other European industrialized nations. All across America, millions of citizens lost their jobs, homes and farms. These people worried that they could not feed their families. With high unemployment, some Americans turned to crime to make a living.

In 1932, Franklin Delano Roosevelt – his name was usually shortened to just FDR – stepped into the job of United States president. He promised to give Americans jobs, food and, most of all, hope for the future. He worked hard to keep this promise as America struggled through the 1930s. By early 1942, factories were running and people were working again, mainly because America was becoming involved in World War II. Americans, at home and abroad, helped win the war. As the 1940s came to a close, Americans once again enjoyed peace and prosperity.

Most of the events in this book took place during Roosevelt's life. On pages that describe events that happened in his lifetime but were not directly connected to him, there are yellow boxes that tell you what he and his family were doing at the time.

THE LAST OF THE GOOD TIMES

"Ours is a land...filled with happy homes; blessed with comfort and opportunity. I have no fears for the future of our country. It is bright with hope." Herbert Hoover spoke these words. He summed up the mood of the country as he became president of the United States on 4 March 1929.

The 1920s had been great years. Most Americans who wanted a job could have one. One out of every five Americans owned a car. Everyone went to the cinema, often two or three times a week. Charlie Chaplin and Mae West were the stars of Hollywood. Babe Ruth was the biggest star in baseball. Charles Lindbergh became the first pilot to fly solo non-stop across the Atlantic Ocean.

FDR

Franklin Delano Roosevelt grew up in Hyde Park, New York. At the age of 29, he was a state **senator**. At 31, President Woodrow Wilson chose him to be assistant **Secretary of the Navy**. Roosevelt enjoyed working in government.

In 1921, Roosevelt's courage was put to the test. At the age of 39, he got a disease called infantile paralysis, or polio. He could not move his legs. They were paralysed. Doctors told him to exercise to keep the disease from getting worse. FDR built up his strength by swimming for hours at a time. He wore leg braces and used a cane. He often needed a wheelchair. None of this stopped FDR from following his dreams. In 1928, he was elected governor of New York.

▼ Roosevelt was governor of the most populated state. His office was in the state **capital**: Albany, New York. Roosevelt sat in a wheelchair made from a kitchen chair.

Franklin D. Roosevelt
FDR was born on 30 January 1882. He grew up in a large, smart house in Hyde Park, New York. He attended college and law school. His cousin Theodore became president of the United States in 1901. From that time, Franklin was interested in government. Franklin married his distant cousin, Eleanor Roosevelt, in 1905. They had five children: Anna, James, Elliot, Franklin, Jr, and John.

Governor Roosevelt

Many New Yorkers were enjoying the good life of the 1920s. However, Roosevelt knew that not all New Yorkers were doing well. He investigated the problems of New York farmers and factory workers. He suggested programmes to improve their schools, lower their **taxes** and provide less expensive electricity.

▶◀ In the 1920s, some Americans earned money by selling goods from barrows (above left) or working in factories (above right). Others were farmers, like the couple in the photograph left. By 1929, many farmers were starving, as their crops failed, and their workers left for better-paying jobs in cities.

▼ This photograph was taken in 1932. It includes Franklin (seated bottom left) and Eleanor, their children, grandchildren and Franklin's mother, Sara.

▼ Many Americans became rich during the 1920s. Some owned large businesses called corporations. Others ran banks that lent money to build houses.

PANIC IN THE STOCK MARKET

Americans felt confident about the country's big businesses. Large companies, such as US Steel and American Telephone and Telegraph (AT&T), were making lots of money. Any American could own a part of these rich companies by buying stocks in the companies through the stock market.

Here is how the US **stock market** works. Stocks are shares of a business. They are for sale in the stock market. You might buy a share of stock for $10. If the company becomes successful, your share could be worth more money. You could sell that stock or hold it to see if it is worth more tomorrow. In the late 1920s, the prices of many stocks kept getting higher. It seemed easy to make money in the stock market. Millions of Americans bought stocks. Many of them borrowed money from banks to buy more stocks.

In late autumn of 1929, stock prices started to fall. A $10 share of stock might have been worth $5. People rushed to sell their stocks before they lost too much money. This made stock prices fall further.

▲ This was the front page of *The New York Times* on 30 October 1929. The stock market panic lasted for many weeks. Some people in business and government hoped that things would improve. But, by the end of 1929, many Americans had lost all their money, their jobs and their homes.

▶ Hard times fall on many Americans. This man who once had a high-paying job now needs money badly. He may have bought this car last year for $300. Today, he will be lucky to sell it for $50. Few people can afford to buy cars. Most of the motor car manufacturers have stopped making new cars.

▶ This man is called a trader. He buys and sells stocks. On 24 October 1929, he will gamble by buying stocks during the panic. Stock prices are very low. They may rise soon. But they could drop lower. Then, on 29 October, the stock market crashes. There are no buyers for stocks. Stock owners have gone broke.

Prices tumble , the market 'crashes'

On 29 October 1929, every shareholder tried to sell their stocks. Almost no one wanted to buy them. The stocks became worthless. People who had used their life savings to buy stocks now had no money. People who had borrowed money from banks to buy stocks were now in **debt**. Most people could not afford to buy new products. So, many companies closed down or at least produced less. They sacked their workers. Millions of Americans now had no jobs.

▶ Stock exchanges are places where stocks are bought and sold. The Stock Exchange on Wall Street in New York City is one of the most important. On 29 October 1929, many shareholders called the Stock Exchange, trying to sell their stocks. Outside, crowds gathered awaiting news of the market crash, as in the photo above.

HARD TIMES

America's good times ended quickly. The nation's finances were in trouble. Then, the stock market collapsed in 1929. People lost their savings and then their jobs and their homes. The hard times lasted until 1939. These years are called the Great Depression.

The **stock market** crash signalled the start of the Great **Depression**. America's factories were over-producing. Machines worked at such great speed that goods were produced faster than people could buy them. By 1929, unsold goods were piling up. Companies started to produce less. They let some of their employees go and put others on part-time work. When people lost their income, they bought even less. Companies sold fewer goods. Many had to close down. By 1932, one out of every three Americans was unemployed, or out of work.

▶ When people heard about the bank failures, they ran to get their money. Those who arrived late found the bank doors locked. By winter of 1932–1933, about 5,000 banks had closed. Nine million people lost their savings. Today the government **insures** bank accounts so that this will not happen again.

FDR versus Hoover
As New York's governor, Franklin Roosevelt had new ideas to help New Yorkers. He started programmes to put people back to work. He created jobs planting trees and improving farm land. Many Americans thought President Herbert Hoover should use these ideas throughout the country. President Hoover disagreed. "People must fight their own battles in their own communities," he said.

10

Banks close too

During the good times of the 1920s, people saved their money at banks. Many banks used most of their customers' savings to buy stocks. The banks lost this money when the stock market crashed. Banks had another problem. Many people had borrowed money from banks. When the Depression started, people could not pay back their loans. As a result, hundreds of banks ran out of money and closed. People could not get back their savings.

◀ Many Americans were too poor to buy food. They stood in '**bread lines**' to get free food. This photo was taken in February 1932 in New York City.

◀ This farmer is giving up on his fields. People can only pay a few cents for a sackful of corn. It is not worth harvesting.

▶ This man once owned a clothing business. Now he worries that he will never earn another dollar. He worries most about his children. There is not enough food for them to eat every day.

◀ Some people lost their homes because they could not pay their **mortgage**. They wandered to a poor section of town and built shacks out of wooden boxes, as here in Seattle, Washington. People called these areas Hoovervilles. They blamed President Hoover for their troubles.

President Roosevelt

Millions of Americans were jobless, homeless and feeling hopeless. Could the country that had grown so strong now collapse? Americans looked to their government leaders for help. President Hoover believed the government should not get involved. In 1932, Franklin Roosevelt ran for president.

Ban on alcohol ends
In December 1933, **Prohibition** ended with the 21st **Amendment**. Roosevelt was in favour of the amendment. Many Americans argued that Prohibition took away personal freedom. Also, the liquor industry could create jobs and raise tax. The 21st Amendment repealed, or cancelled, the 18th Amendment for Prohibition.

▲ This photo was taken in October 1932 in Indianapolis, Indiana. Roosevelt is running for president against the current president, Herbert Hoover. During the 1932 campaign, Roosevelt visited 38 of the 48 states. He travelled 43,400 km, many of them on a train called 'the Roosevelt Special'. Roosevelt won the **election** by seven million votes.

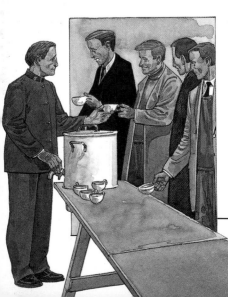

◄ Many people were embarrassed to stand in line for free food. But jobs in the New Deal programmes paid only $30 to $50 a month, which was not enough to house and feed a family. Communities set up **soup kitchens** to feed hungry people.

Roosevelt promised Americans a 'new deal'. He would help create government programmes so that people could make money and support themselves again. Roosevelt won the presidential **election** in 1932 and at his **inauguration** he gave America hope by saying, "This great nation will endure.... The only thing we have to fear is fear itself."

President Roosevelt called on **Congress** to get his ideas going quickly. The new programmes paid people to develop parks and to build roads, schools and hydroelectric dams. Farmers received money to run their farms again. Roosevelt wanted people to earn money so they could buy goods. Then the factories could re-open and hire more people.

New Hope
Roosevelt's **New Deal** did not end the **Depression**. But it gave many Americans jobs, homes and – most of all – new confidence in America's businesses and government. Many New Deal programmes continued for more than 65 years and are important parts of America today. They include minimum wage laws and Social Security payments (for Americans who are too old or not able to work).

▲ Farmland in the Tennessee River valley was poor. Scientists developed fertilizers to make the soil better.

Informing the people

President Roosevelt regularly talked to the American people over the radio during 'fireside chats'. He explained how he planned to improve things. "He said he understood what we were going through," remembers Rachel Hasson, whose parents owned a grocery store in Los Angeles, California. "For many years, his fireside chats made us feel that everything would be OK."

◄ One of the biggest projects of the New Deal took place in the Tennessee River valley. The river often flooded. In 1933, the Tennessee Valley Authority (TVA) hired workers to build 40 **dams** along the river and its branches. The dams stopped flooding and created cheap electric power.

▲ Roosevelt gives a fireside chat.

THE DUST BOWL

The Dust Bowl of the 1930s

Dear Mrs Roosevelt: "For the first time of my lifetime I am asking a favour. Among your friends, do you know of one who is discarding a spring coat? If so could you beg the old one for me? We were hit very hard by the drought and every penny we can save goes [for the crops]."

This letter was sent on 10 May 1935, from a farm woman from Goff, Kansas, part of America's Dust Bowl. This region got its name during a seven-year drought in the 1930s. A drought means there was very little rain. In the 1920s, farmers had unwisely ploughed up hectares of grassland to plant wheat. By 1934, there were no grassy roots to hold the soil down. There was no rain to keep it down either. Then the wind storms came.

▼ ▲ This family is fixing its car as they prepare to move out of the Dust Bowl, leaving their land and their home. The father and oldest son hope to get work on farms further west. In 1935 alone, about 40 big storms had swept across their land.

Clouds of dust

Whenever the wind blew through the Dust Bowl, the soil lifted up from the fields. It blew across the land in a thick dusty cloud. Cattle choked. People suffered lung damage. Cars' engines and farm machines were ruined.

Moving out

Farmers in the Dust Bowl felt hopeless. Thousands of families decided to leave their farms for good. Some packed up and went to big cities. Many headed to California. They hoped to find jobs on farms and a better life there. However, there were many more new arrivals to California than there were jobs for them.

Help to farmers

The president and **Congress** tried to help farmers through these bad times. They passed laws to give **relief** money to families in the Dust Bowl. They passed the Agricultural Adjustment Act whereby farmers in other regions were paid not to grow certain crops. Fewer crops meant people had to pay higher prices for food.

▲ A Dust Bowl scene. This photo was taken at Dallas, South Dakota, on 13 May 1936. Millions of tons of soil turned to dust and blew all the way to the East Coast. Sailors 32 km off the coast in the Atlantic Ocean said they swept Dust Bowl dust off the decks of their ship.

YEARS OF DUST

RESETTLEMENT ADMINISTRATION
Rescues Victims
Restores Land to Proper Use

◀ This poster was created for the US government by Ben Shahn. Many writers and artists created works about the Dust Bowl struggles. John Steinbeck wrote a famous novel called *The Grapes of Wrath*. Songwriter Woody Guthrie (who wrote *This Land Is Your Land*) wrote *Hard Travelling* about the farmers who left the Dust Bowl.

Changes on reservations
For about 100 years, the US government operated Native American **reservations** where Native American religions were banned. In 1934, the government ended this policy and said Native Americans could live according to their traditions. Congress also passed the Indian Reorganization Act. It protected the land on Native American reservations from development.

WORK PROGRAMMES

It cost millions of dollars to create new jobs. It would have been cheaper to simply give people money. But Roosevelt said: "Most Americans want to give something for what they get.... Honest work is the saving barrier between them and moral disintegration."

In May 1935, the government set up the Works Progress Administration (WPA). It came up with 'small useful projects'. Some workers repaired pavements and roads. Others built playgrounds.

The WPA gave work to artists, actors, musicians and writers. Artists painted **murals** and carved statues for public buildings. Actors staged operas and puppet shows. Musicians performed concerts. Writers created guidebooks for every state. About 8,500,000 people got jobs through the WPA

▼ The government paid artists to paint pictures to brighten up buildings. Some of these paintings hang in the White House and can still be seen in other public buildings.

▼ This artist, Alfred Castagne, was paid by the WPA to make a sketch of these workers. The workers were paid by the WPA to build curbs on a street in Michigan.

▼ This was a recruitment poster for the Civilian Conservation Corps (CCC). Between 1933 and 1942, this organization gave work and training in forestry, farming, flood control and clearing up to more than 2,500,000 young people. The poster was designed by the Illinois WPA Art Project.

A YOUNG MAN'S OPPORTUNITY

CCC

FOR WORK PLAY STUDY & HEALTH

APPLICATIONS TAKEN BY
ILLINOIS EMERGENCY RELIEF COMMISSION
ILLINOIS SELECTING AGENCY

The 1936 election

Roosevelt ran for president again in 1936 and won. In his second **inauguration** speech, he said: "The test of our progress is not whether we add more to the abundance of those who have much; it is whether we provide enough for those who have too little."

Critics

Not everyone loved FDR and his ideas. Many people criticized the **New Deal** programmes. The government did not have the money to pay the workers in all the new programmes. The government spent more than it had and it was in **debt**. It raised some **taxes** to ease the situation. Other critics said the programmes favoured workers, but were unfair to big business owners. Still other critics feared that people would get used to government handouts. They would not want to seek jobs in private firms again.

▼ Many of today's roads, airports and parks were built as WPA projects. By 1940, the WPA had constructed or rebuilt 200,000 buildings and bridges and 965,000 km of roads and water pipes (below left). Some WPA jobs were as small as sawing wood (below right). Poor people received the wood to burn for heat.

◄ Some WPA workers, like these women, sewed clothing. Others canned vegetables or made books and maps in Braille for blind people. The WPA was run by Frances Perkins, Roosevelt's Secretary for Labour. She was the first woman to hold a senior government job.

A WPA PROJECT

BUILDING THE TALLEST AND LONGEST

Americans have always had grand ideas – wanting to move faster, fly further and communicate better. Some of America's grand plans stalled during the Depression. Other plans became reality and set new records, both for America and the world.

During the rich days of the 1920s, a group of builders dreamed up New York City's Empire State Building. By the time construction was completed in 1931, the **Depression** was under way. Businesses were closing. Few people wanted to rent office space in the world's tallest building. Some people jokingly called it the 'Empty State Building' – in the same way as Londoners described the Canary Wharf Tower in the 1980s.

Despite the empty offices, the 102-storey building amazed people. At 381 m high, it seemed like a real 'skyscraper'. It towered over the rest of New York City. Anyone who could afford a spare dollar queued to take the lift to the top floors to look down upon the toy-size city below.

Golden Gate Bridge

In 1937, builders in San Francisco, California, built the longest bridge in the world. The 2,722 m bridge spanned the entrance of San Francisco Bay. The bridge has a six-lane road that helps people travel from northern California to the peninsula of San Francisco. Many bridges have been built since 1937. The Golden Gate Bridge is still one of the longest suspension bridges and is a major tourist attraction.

▶ In the 1930s, many people wanted to travel by derigible. On 6 May 1937, the German-built *Hindenburg* exploded while docking in Lakehurst, New Jersey. Thirty-five of the 97 passengers died.

▼ This photograph, by Lewis Hine, was taken while the Empire State Building was under construction. In the 1970s, it was overtaken in height with the construction of the 412 m World Trade Center in New York City and the 443 m Sears Tower in Chicago, Illinois. Canary Wharf Tower is 244 m high.

◀ Photographers soar by San Francisco's Golden Gate Bridge in a small aeroplane. They get a bird's-eye view of the construction of the world's longest bridge at that time.

▲ The Grand Coulee **Dam** is the largest concrete dam in the US. It was built from 1934 to 1942 and spans the Columbia River in Washington State.

▼ In 1936, the McDonnell Douglas company began making passenger planes for Trans World Airlines (TWA). Each plane carried 21 passengers. The passenger aircraft could travel across the country in less than 24 hours, but had to stop several times for fuel.

19

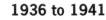

MAKING A LIVING

The Depression changed the lives of many Americans. People who had once been rich took jobs polishing shoes and planting trees. They spent money only on necessities: food, shelter and medicine. Even when times got better, these people saved their money. They had trouble treating themselves to a new pair of shoes or a meal in a restaurant.

Children knew they were living in tough times. Some went out to work at the age of 13 so they could give money to their families. Most children had to make do with home-made, improvised toys. Scraps of fabrics were made into dolls. A mass of string became a ball. Children got used to wearing extra-big clothing. Parents bought clothes that were too large so children would not grow out of them too soon.

Eleanor Roosevelt
Most Americans admired the president's wife, the nation's 'first lady', Eleanor Roosevelt. Since she could travel more easily than the president, she went around the country talking to people and checking on government projects.

Eleanor visited workers in coal mines and spoke to people in unemployment queues. People called her the 'eyes and ears of the president'. She also wrote a newspaper column and had her own radio programme. She was more active than any other first lady before her.

▶ Mrs Roosevelt spent most of her life helping people. In this photo, taken in New York in 1932, she is serving food at a **soup kitchen**. She also visited hospitals, schools and factories.

> **Another election**
> It was time for another presidential **election** in 1940. FDR already had served two terms. No other president ever tried to serve more. Critics said that it was time for a change. Modifying a quote used by Abraham Lincoln during the 1864 elections, FDR said: "Don't change horses in midstream." Franklin Roosevelt won the election for a third time.

▼ In the 1930s, nine million workers belonged to **unions** so they could fight for better pay and working conditions. These are workers from Ford Motor Company.

▼ People who managed to keep their jobs lived comfortably. Rent in a housing development in Washington, DC, was $20 to $45 a month. People who had money could buy goods at low '**Depression**' prices. This family has a modern electric cooker, which became popular in the 1930s.

◄ Mechanical refrigerators (far left) became popular in the 1920s, but every few years a bigger and better model was introduced. Automatic washing machines (left) were a new household convenience introduced in 1937. They saved hours of time spent washing each piece of clothing by hand.

21

TAKING A BREAK

Americans wanted relief from the worries of the Depression. They often turned to a large wooden box in the living room: the radio. In the 1930s, two out of every three homes had a radio. That was double the number of homes with telephones.

Families gathered around a radio the way families today watch television. Radios brought major league baseball teams, such as the Brooklyn Dodgers and Boston Braves, into millions of homes. Radios also brought world news, as a major war brewed in Europe. Most of all, radios brought lively entertainment. There were music shows, played by live bands. There were comedy shows with George Burns, Gracie Allen and Jack Benny. Like many radio stars, these people later became TV stars.

▼ In 1936, a writer named Margaret Mitchell wrote *Gone With the Wind*. This romantic **Civil War** story became the best-selling book in America. In 1939, the story was made into the longest movie of the 1930s (3 hours). It also made the most money. The film's leading female actress, Vivien Leigh, was English. She played the part of Scarlet O'Hara.

▼ Americans could not seem to get enough of baseball. The first All-Star Game was played in Comiskey Park in Chicago on 6 July 1933. The Baseball Hall of Fame opened in Cooperstown, New York, in 1939. Babe Ruth, Lou Gehrig, Joe DiMaggio and Dizzy Dean were American baseball heroes of the time.

America's favourites:
1931 the film *Dracula*
1932 game of Monopoly created by Charles B. Darrow
1933 film *King Kong*
1933 first comic book: *Funnies on Parade*
1936 book *Uncle Tom's Cabin*, written in the 1850s, is a best-seller
1937 the first full-length animated film, Walt Disney's *Snow White and the Seven Dwarfs*
1937 first *Bugs Bunny* cartoon
1938 first *Superman* action comic book
1940 M&M candies first sold

In new screen splendor...
The most magnificent picture ever!

DAVID O. SELZNICK'S PRODUCTION OF MARGARET MITCHELL'S
"GONE WITH THE WIND"

◀ African American Jesse Owens was the star of the 1936 Olympics in Berlin, Germany. Owens won four gold medals in track and field. This annoyed many Germans, who believed black people were inferior.

Movies

Americans also loved to escape to the cinema. In 1938, almost 80 million cinema tickets were bought each week. For 25 cents, you could watch a film, a cartoon, a **newsreel** and eat two boxes of sweets. In 1939, *The Wizard of Oz* was one of America's favourite films. It tells of a girl's escape from a Kansas farm during the **Depression**. She arrives in the colourful land of Oz and later realizes 'there's no place like home'. Like most films then, there was a happy ending.

Americans also enjoyed watching happy films with child stars Shirley Temple and Mickey Rooney. There was also the comedy of the Marx Brothers and the suspense created by Alfred Hitchcock.

◀ The radio was an important piece of furniture. It was the focal point of every home. Everyone had a favourite show. Children ran home from school to listen to radio adventure stories. Millions of women tuned into dramatic tales filled with joy and tears. Soap companies advertised during these programmes, giving them the name 'soap operas'. Programmes lasted between 15 and 60 minutes.

WORLD WAR II BEGINS IN EUROPE

When World War I ended in 1918, it was called the 'war to end all wars'. But peace did not last. German people were angry. Germany had lost land in that war. Germany's government owed money to other countries for war damages. By 1930, German people had more problems because the Depression hit Germany too.

Thousands of Germans were jobless and homeless. They wanted a strong leader to end their troubles. A former soldier named Adolf Hitler made public speeches, saying he could make Germany great again. Hitler became Germany's leader in 1933. He turned out to be a very dangerous leader. He made himself a **dictator** and took total control of the government. He blamed such groups as Jews, immigrants and disabled people for Germany's problems. Soon he had these people arrested and sent to prisons called **concentration camps**.

FDR plans for war
The president felt America would need to help Britain and France stop Hitler. On 6 January 1941, he spoke to Americans: "No nation could remain either safe or free unless protected by a united world order founded on 'four essential freedoms': freedom of speech, freedom of worship, freedom from want and freedom from fear." FDR asked **Congress** for money to buy **military** weapons and supplies.

▲ German U-boats (submarines) tried to destroy American supply ships before they reached Europe. This is the view of a supply ship through the lens of the U-boat periscope. In September of 1940, U-boats sank 27 **Allied** ships in the Atlantic.

▲ Adolf Hitler ruled Germany as a dictator from 1933 to 1945. He ordered millions of people killed because he felt they threatened his power.

▲ Benito Mussolini ruled Italy for 21 years, most of them as a dictator. In 1940, he sent his soldiers to join Hitler's soldiers in taking over France.

▼ In 1936, Italy, Germany and Japan agreed to join forces. They called themselves Axis Powers. Britain and France, soon joined by the Soviet Union and other countries, were called Allies. This map shows Europe in September 1939 when the war began.

World War II in Europe by 1943

Allied areas
Axis countries
Axis occupied areas
Neutral countries

Norway, Sweden, Finland, Estonia, Latvia, Lithuania, Denmark, United Kingdom, Eire, Netherlands, Belgium, Germany, Poland, Normandy, Brittany, Czechoslovakia, Switzerland, Austria, Hungary, Romania, France, Yugoslavia, Soviet Union, Italy, Bulgaria, Albania, Portugal, Spain, Sicily, Greece, Turkey, Morocco, Tunisia, Syria, Lebanon, Iraq, Algeria, Libya, Egypt, Palestine, Saudi Arabia

The road to war

Hitler and his party, called **Nazis**, took control of Germany. They outlawed freedom of the press. They forbade people to move, change jobs or to travel without permission. They began training young Germans aged 6 to 18 to be loyal German soldiers. They taught children to spy on their families and to report parents who spoke against the Nazis.

Then Hitler set out to control the world. In 1938 and 1939, he took over Austria and Czechoslovakia. In September 1939, he took over Poland. France and Britain wanted to help Poland. They declared war on Germany. World War II began.

▲ This photo was taken in Warsaw in Poland in 1940. Starting in 1939, all Jews in Germany and Poland had to wear a yellow Star of David sewn onto their clothes so the police could watch their movements.

▶ By 1941, Britain had run out of money and ships. She was fighting alone – a small island against a Europe now occupied by Germany. America began sending aeroplanes, ships and weapons to Britain. The ships in the background are called Liberty ships. They were made in the United States and sailed to Europe across the Atlantic Ocean. The ship in front is an American destroyer.

25

UNITED STATES AT WAR

Winston Churchill, Britain's prime minister, was listening to the 9 P.M. radio news on 7 December 1941. With great surprise, he ran to call President Roosevelt. "What's this about Japan?" Churchill asked. "It's quite true," said FDR. "They have attacked us at Pearl Harbour. We are all in the same boat now."

In the 1930s and 1940s, Japan attacked and took over parts of China and south-east Asia (later called Vietnam, Cambodia and Laos). As punishment, the United States and Britain stopped selling oil and other goods to Japan. Japan's leaders, Emperor Hirohito and Hideki Tojo, resented this interference. Tojo decided to stop the United States with **military** force. His air force bombed the American naval base in Pearl Harbour, Hawaii. Nineteen US ships and 150 planes were destroyed and about 2,400 people were killed.

▼ The Pearl Harbour attack made Americans fearful of the Japanese Americans who lived in the US. In March 1942, FDR ordered more than 110,000 Japanese Americans living on the West Coast to sell their homes and move to special camps.

▲ Hideki Tojo was a military leader. In 1941, he became Japan's premier (government leader). On 6 December 1941, FDR wrote to Tojo asking that "our two great countries... restore traditional [friendship] and prevent further destruction in the world". The next day Tojo ordered the attack on Pearl Harbour.

FDR speaks
On 8 December, FDR spoke to an emergency session of **Congress**. "Yesterday, 7 December 1941...the United States of America was attacked by naval and air forces of the Empire of Japan. Always will we remember the character of the attack against us. ...[We will] make very certain that this form of treachery shall never endanger us again. With confidence in our armed forces – with the unbounded determination of our people – we will gain the inevitable triumph – so help us God." Then the president asked Congress to declare war on Japan. In just 33 minutes, it was done.

Joining the war

FDR heard about the Pearl Harbour attack in a call from the **Secretary of the Navy**. FDR's advisors ran to the White House. The President immediately prepared a message to the nation. The next day, the US Congress declared war on Japan. Britain and Canada did the same. Three days later, Japan's friends – Germany and Italy – declared war on the United States. For the second time in 25 years, America was at war. Americans were ready to help. Thousands rushed to sign up for military service. Factories that had been closed during the **Depression** opened their doors again. They began making tanks, guns, planes and ammunition. Factories needed workers again. The Depression was over!

The early war years
1939
Sept. 1 Germany invades Poland
Sept. 3 Britain and France declare war on Germany; World War II begins
1940
April Germany takes over Denmark and Norway
May Germany takes over Holland and Belgium
June German army marches into Paris. France surrenders
July–October Germany bombs Britain, but the RAF defeats its air force; Japan joins **Axis Powers**
1941
June Germany invades the Soviet Union; Soviet Union joins the Allied Powers;
Dec. Japan bombs Pearl Harbour, Hawaii; US enters the war

◀ On Sunday morning, 7 December 1941, US battleships were lined up in Pearl Harbour, Hawaii. At 7:55 A.M., Japanese planes flew overhead and dropped bombs. This picture shows sailors trying to rescue the crew of the battleship *West Virginia*.

THE U·S·MARINES
WANT YOU
ENLIST TODAY

◀ This 1942 poster encouraged Americans to join the **Marines**. Five million Americans volunteered for military service. Ten million were conscripted. That means the government required them to serve.

27

REPORTING FOR DUTY

When the United States joined the war, the Allied countries cheered. They knew that America was the world's richest nation. It had plenty of factories, people and resources such as steel. America's navy would become the largest in the world.

In 1943, over 2,500,000 men and women joined the US **military** service. Most left for Britain, Italy, northern Africa and the Pacific islands on ocean liners. Life as a soldier took great courage. No matter how often they faced the enemy's guns, the soldiers never got used to combat. They fought through hunger, cold and fear for many reasons. They loved their country. They hated the enemies of freedom. Most of all, they felt responsible for their fellow soldiers and would not let them down.

▼ President Roosevelt (right) met with Britain's **Prime Minister** Winston Churchill in August 1941. They planned their goals for fighting the **Axis Powers**. They signed the **Atlantic Charter**.

▶ More than 15 million men and 300,000 women served in the US armed forces during WWII.
1. About 2,411,000 served in the Army Air Force.
2. About a million African Americans served in WWII. Rarely were they **segregated** from white members. Many of them worked as mechanics.
3. Soldiers were often called GIs because their equipment was stamped GI meaning 'Government Issue'.
4. Over 3,400,000 men and women served as sailors on US ships.
5. Over 40,000 women served on air bases.

1. Pilot

2. Mechanic

3. GI

Fighting around the world

Americans joined **Allied** troops in North Africa and Europe, and on islands in the Pacific. In Europe, the Germans seemed unbeatable. They had taken over most of the continent. Their submarines sank ships faster than the Allies could replace them. In North Africa, US, British and free-French troops led by General Dwight Eisenhower took over Morocco and Algeria. They trapped German troops led by General Erwin Rommel in Tunisia. By May 1943, the Allies had won in North Africa.

In the Pacific, Americans faced Japanese troops on islands such as Guadalcanal, Guam, Iwo Jima and New Guinea. Allied forces won important Pacific victories, particularly at the Battle of Midway, when American planes sank four Japanese aircraft carriers.

▼ On Pacific islands, American troops faced not only stifling heat, poisonous insects and deadly diseases, but also skilled Japanese soldiers who would rather die fighting than **surrender**.

4. Sailor   **5. Air Force Women**

▲ American factories stopped making motor cars and radios and began making tanks and planes. This equipment helped the Allies win World War II (often shortened to WWII or called the Second World War). This is a photo of an American-made Stuart tank rolling through North Africa in 1942.

THE HOME FRONT

America needed all its citizens to help win the war. While millions of men left home to fight, millions of women stepped into their jobs. Some assembled planes. Others took over local jobs, such as driving buses and serving petrol.

The war affected every American family. Farmers grew more food than ever. The government bought it and sent it to its soldiers and sailors. That made food scarce for everyone at home. The government set a limit on how much sugar, butter, coffee and meat each fami could buy every month. Millions of Americans planted 'victory gardens' in their backyards and even on city roofto These gardens fed their families while t government sent food overseas.

Shortages and reusing metals

There were other shortages on the home front. Tyre factories stopped making car tyres so they could make tyres for buses. People had to patch anc repatch their old tyres. The **military** als needed petrol. Citizens could only get limited amounts of petrol for their cars.

Shoe factories stopped making shoes and made military boots instead. Dress factories made US Army, Navy and Air Force uniforms. Few people bought new clothes during the war. A trade developed in second-hand goods. The government asked Americans to collect scrap metal for the weapons factories. Citizens turned over toothpaste tubes, old lawn mowers, bicycles and licence plates.

▼ The government gave every family ration books, or food allowance, stamps like these. At food shops, you could use a stamp to buy 450 g of sugar every two weeks.

War and the White House

Before war broke out, Franklin and Eleanor Roosevelt entertained frequently at the White House. They had 13 grandchildren, who often stayed with them. An indoor swimming pool was installed in the White House so that FDR could exercise. After the US entered the war, the Roosevelts did little entertaining. They both frequently travelled. Their four sons went to war. Worried about enemy attacks on the White House and the president, workers installed machine guns on the White House roof. They built a **bomb shelter** in the basement.

▶ This poster encouraged women to help their country by going to work.

▼ America's factories ran day and night. Americans made 300,000 warplanes at a cost of $45 billion.

We Can Do It!

What things cost in 1943
- loaf of bread: 9 cents
- 5 litres of petrol: 17 cents
- *Time* magazine: 10 cents
- toothpaste: 37 cents
- bottle of soda: 5 cents
- postcard: 1 cent
- airmail stamp: 8 cents
- room for one night at a New York City hotel (with bathroom and radio): $2.50

▲ To keep factories running, five million women took jobs. Advertising posters with pictures of a character called Rosie the Riveter encouraged women to go to work. Thousands of 'Rosies' attached aeroplane parts with fasteners called rivets.

▲ The government paid women and men the same for the same work. However, many employers found ways to pay women less. After the war, many women left their jobs to become housewives. Others were sacked to make jobs available for returning soldiers.

31

ATTACK ON EUROPE

While Americans listened to war news on the radio, Europeans listened to bombs and gunfire outside their homes. In June 1940, Germany conquered France. That August, they began bombing England's major cities. In June 1941, Hitler attacked the Soviet Union. That may have been his costliest mistake.

Roosevelt battles on
By 1944, Franklin Roosevelt is tired and ill. Still, he campaigns for a fourth term as president and wins. His war efforts are popular with Americans. No other president has served this long and never will again. Passed in 1951, the 22nd **Amendment** limits any president to two consecutive terms.

For 18 months, the Germans successfully stormed through the **Soviet Union**. But the Soviet army gathered its strength and finally ended the **invasion** at Stalingrad. In the winter of 1943, they cut off the German supply lines. German soldiers were freezing and starving to death. That February, the Germans finally left the Soviet Union. Hitler's army never again won another major battle.

On to North Africa and Italy
By May 1943, the **Allies** forced the last **Axis** soldiers out of North Africa. On 10 July 1943, the Allies invaded Sicily, an Italian island between North Africa and mainland Italy. They arrived by air and sea. From there they invaded the Italian mainland. The Italian people were sick of the war. They overthrew their leader Mussolini and put their king back in power. The new government surrendered to the Allies on 3 September 1943, but the war in Italy carried on.

▶ American troops enter the city of Palermo in Sicily. On 3 September 1943, the US Army crossed from Sicily to Italy's mainland. The Italian government surrendered and soon declared war on Germany. German soldiers still occupied much of Italy. Allied soldiers fought their way north to the **capital**, Rome, and took control of it in June 1944.

▼ US bomber planes try to destroy Germany's weapons factories and railways. This will not be easy. German radar can spot these planes and anti-aircraft guns try to shoot them out of the sky.

▶ Fighting on the Pacific islands continued. This photo shows United States **Marines** storming ashore at Tarawa in the Gilbert Islands on 20 November 1943.

Bombing Germany

The Allies moved east towards Germany. Tanks and trucks drove overland. Planes buzzed through the skies over German cities. American planes dropped bombs all day. The British dropped bombs at night. At first, Germans shot down many of the bombers and quickly repaired their factories. Eventually, the bombs were too much for Germany. The Allies had destroyed most of the weapons factories. Millions of Germans lost their homes or their lives in the bombings.

▲ General George Patton, Jr led American troops in the invasion of North Africa and the capture of Sicily.

▲ General Douglas MacArthur led the US Army in the South Pacific. His troops freed the Philippine Islands.

VICTORY IN EUROPE

The Allies had a plan. Troops would cross the English Channel from England to Normandy, France. From there, they would move into France and get rid of the enemy. The invasion began 6 June 1944 – D-Day. Andy Rooney was there and wrote this passage (printed at the top of the opposite page) in his book, *My War*:

▼ Photographer Robert F. Sargent took this picture in Normandy, France, on D-Day.

◄ On D-Day, 2,700 ships crossed the English Channel, filled with tanks, guns, and soldiers mainly from America, Britain, and Canada. The Germans did not expect them to land in Normandy.

"No one can tell the story of D-Day because no one knows it. Each of the 60,000 men who waded ashore that day knew a little part of the story too well. Each knew a friend shot through the throat, shot through the knee....
In **Allied** Headquarters in England, the war directors were exultant [happy]. They saw no blood, no dead, no dying. From the **statistician's** point of view, the **invasion** was a great success."

Moving in

At first, the Normandy invasion went well for the Allies. But one US attack was a disaster. The Germans were firing guns from all directions. Landing craft brought soldiers and tanks close to the beach, only to hit explosive mines buried in the sea. Whole crews drowned as tanks dropped into the water. Luckily, by nightfall, the surviving Allies managed to get ashore and move into France.

By August 1944, the Allies pushed the Germans out of most of north-western France. On August 25, the Allies marched into Paris, the French **capital**, and took over the city. France was free!

◀ In August 1944, Allied troops captured St Malo, Brittany, in north-western France. This photo shows a US anti-tank gun.

End of the war in Europe
3 Sept. 1943 Italy surrenders
6 June 1944 D-Day invasion of Normandy
25 Aug. 1944 France is liberated, or set free
7 May 1945 Germany surrenders
8 May 1945 Victory in Europe (VE) Day

Germany's defeat

American, British and Canadian soldiers pushed through France into Germany. Meanwhile, **Soviet Union** troops pushed the German soldiers out of Poland and moved into Germany. Hitler knew he was defeated. Because he wanted to be the world's most powerful leader but had failed, he killed himself on 30 April 1945. On 7 May, Germany **surrendered**.

◀ This cover of a US Army magazine shows a Parisian woman helping American soldiers to speak French. The soldiers have just **liberated** Paris.

SHUTTLE-BOMBING BETWEEN THE U.K. AND RUSSIA

THE HOLOCAUST

As Allied soldiers moved into Europe, they saw the horror of Hitler's power. Hitler had ordered his troops to take millions of people to death camps. The Allied soldiers found these camps filled with starving survivors and millions of dead bodies. The destruction of Jews in particular is called the Holocaust.

Franklin Roosevelt dies
FDR died on 12 April 1945 in Warm Springs, Georgia. As his body was taken to the Washington-bound train, his Warm Springs friends lined up their wheelchairs and waved goodbye. After his funeral in Washington, he was buried at his home in Hyde Park, New York. Vice-president Harry S. Truman became president.

In the early 1900s, Jews played a major role in European countries. They were doctors, lawyers, bankers, shopkeepers, writers and musicians. Hitler, however, thought Jews were evil. He believed his people – white northern Europeans – were superior. As soon as Hitler became Germany's leader, he ordered his soldiers to round up Jews in Holland, France, Austria, Italy and other countries. Railway carriages filled with Jews headed for the **concentration camps**.

▼ American soldiers **liberate** survivors at a concentration camp in 1945. All the survivors are weak and starving, but thankful. In the camps, strong people were made to work like slaves. The weak were killed in **gas chambers**. The German soldiers had nowhere to bury all the dead so the bodies were burned.

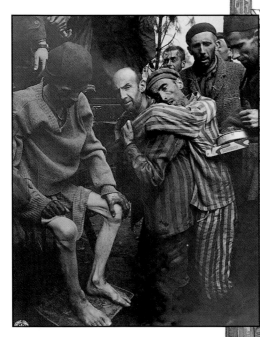

▲ This wartime photograph shows Jews in Wobbelin concentration camp in Poland.

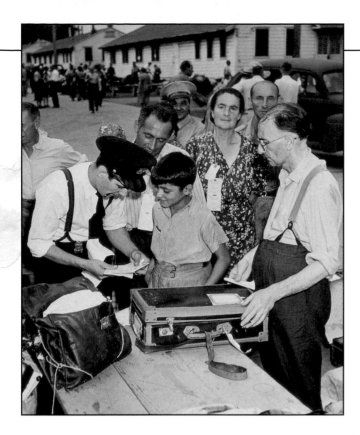

▲ During the 1930s and 1940s, Jews tried to escape Germany and go to the US and friendly European nations such as Britain. However, US **immigration** laws denied them entry. In June 1944, a US government agency managed to get 874 Jews into the country by calling them 'prisoners of war'. The photo shows some of these people at an army base in Oswego, New York. They were kept there until the the war ended in August 1945.

What happened to the survivors?

Two out of every three European Jews died in concentration camps. That is about six million Jews. Hitler's soldiers also tortured and killed millions of Poles, Slavs and Gypsies. The **Allied** countries decided to put **Nazi** leaders on trial. In 1945 and 1946, the Nuremberg Trials sentenced 12 Nazi leaders to death. Many other Nazis went to prison.

About 300,000 Jews survived the concentration camps and tried to start their lives again. Many went to their bombed-out communities to search for parents, sisters, brothers, friends. But most Jews were afraid to stay in Europe. About two-thirds (198,000) left for Palestine. It was called the 'Jewish homeland' and is now known as Israel. Nearly 72,000 Jews went to the United States; 16,000 to Canada; and 1,000 came to Britain.

THE WAR ENDS

On the day he died, Roosevelt was writing a speech. It said, "The work, my friends, is peace. More than an end of this war – an end to the beginnings of all wars. Yes, an end, for ever, to this impractical, unrealistic settlement of the differences between governments by the mass killing of peoples."

FDR did not live to give that speech, but peace arrived just four months after he wrote it. Peace came at a terrible price. Hundreds of thousands of Japanese people died for it.

The war was not over with the victory in Europe in May 1945. The Japanese would not give up. Americans battled the Japanese to take back islands in the Pacific. American bombs destroyed most of the Japanese navy and air force. Some **Allied** leaders wanted to **invade** Japan. That decision would risk the lives of millions of Allied soldiers. President Truman had another option – an entirely new weapon.

▼ Japan had taken over many islands in the Pacific, including the Philippines, which were once controlled by the US. In February 1945, Americans led by General MacArthur took back the Philippines. The United States then introduced a plan called island hopping. This would involve capturing other Japanese-held islands so US forces could get close enough to Japan to launch an invasion. This map shows where major battles took place.

◄ America was succeeding in taking back the Philippines, Iwo Jima, Okinawa and other Pacific islands. Still, the Japanese fought back. In *kamikaze* attacks, Japanese pilots loaded old planes with bombs and deliberately crashed their planes into Allied ships, killing themselves.

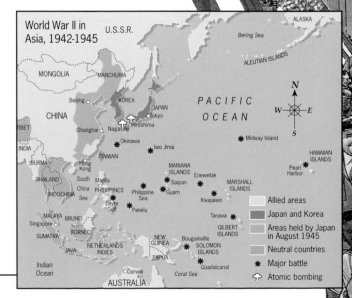

World War II in Asia, 1942-1945

U.S.S.R.
ALASKA
Bering Sea
ALEUTIAN ISLANDS
MONGOLIA
MANCHURIA
PACIFIC OCEAN
Beijing
KOREA
JAPAN
Tokyo
CHINA
Shanghai
Nagasaki
Hiroshima
TIBET
Midway Island
Okinawa
Iwo Jima
INDIA
TAIWAN
BURMA
Hong Kong
MARIANA ISLANDS
Enewetak
HAWAIIAN ISLANDS
THAILAND
South China Sea
Manila
Saipan
MARSHALL ISLANDS
Pearl Harbor
INDOCHINA
PHILIPPINES
Philippine Sea
Guam
Kwajalein
Leyte Gulf
Peleliu
MALAYA
BRUNEI
Tarawa
Singapore
BORNEO
GILBERT ISLANDS
SUMATRA
NETHERLANDS INDIES
NEW GUINEA
Bougainville
SOLOMON ISLANDS
JAVA
PAPUA
Guadalcanal
Indian Ocean
Darwin
Coral Sea
AUSTRALIA

Allied areas
Japan and Korea
Areas held by Japan in August 1945
Neutral countries
✳ Major battle
⚓ Atomic bombing

▼ As the atom bomb exploded on Nagasaki, an enormous fireball filled the sky, followed by a shock wave and heavy winds. This photo shows buildings flattened by the bomb.The bomb's radiation lasted several years and killed 100,000 more people.

Truman's decision

The new weapon was the atomic bomb. It was a powerful weapon that would kill many people and release a long-lasting poison, called **radiation**. Truman spoke to scientists and government leaders to try to make a wise decision. If he dropped the bomb on Japan, thousands of Japanese people would die, including women and children. If the war carried on, thousands of Allied soldiers would die.

On 6 August 1945, an American aeroplane dropped an atomic bomb on the city of Hiroshima. Over 60,000 people died instantly. At least 40,000 more died in the following days. On 9 August, the US dropped a second bomb on the city of Nagasaki, killing 40,000 people and injuring 40,000 as well. Japan could take no more. On 14 August 1945, Japan **surrendered**. World War II was over.

◀ In New York City, millions of Americans joined a celebration parade on V-J Day (Victory over Japan Day) on 2 September 1945. On that day, Japanese officials signed the surrender papers.

▼ This photograph shows American and Japanese officials at the surrender ceremony. It was held aboard the battleship USS *Missouri* in Tokyo Bay. Americans throughout the country listened on the radio.

A CHANGING AMERICA

World War II was over. Soldiers, sailors and pilots returned home. They went back to their jobs and married their sweethearts. There were broken hearts for those who did not return. There were still hard times for those who had always been poor. But for millions of Americans, the good times were back.

After the war, millions of couples started families. Between 1946 and 1960, more than 63 million babies were born in the US – more than double the number in the previous 15 years. Those babies would need homes, schools, clothes, food and entertainment. For years to come, manufacturers would be making products for this group of children. This big jump in the number of births became known as the 'baby boom'.

Many young families wanted a house with a garden and a garage. They no longer needed to live near their offices or factories in the city. They could buy a car and drive to their workplaces from a house outside the city. Hundreds of neighbourhoods sprang up in the **suburbs**. Builders bought farmland and built homes, schools, roads and shops.

▼ After the war, railway companies spent billions to get their war-exhausted trains in shape. But business never picked up. Americans were getting used to travelling by car and plane. This painting by Alexander Leydenfrost shows a 1945 locomotive, *Power*.

▲ Customers no longer stood at a counter and ask for the foods they needed. Now Americans had supermarkets. People walked down aisles and took packages from shelves or out of deep-freezes.

▶ Car factories switched from making tanks to making cars again. In 1949, they produced more cars than ever. It seemed as if everyone was ready for a new car – especially returning soldiers and families who moved to the suburbs.

Working for equality

African Americans could not live in white neighbourhoods or go to white schools. Even America's favourite past-time – baseball – made African Americans play in **Negro** leagues instead of the major leagues. Then, in 1947, African American Jackie Robinson played his first major league game for the Brooklyn Dodgers. Fans and other players shouted rude names at him. He was brave. By the end of that season, he was a star. From that time on, baseball has been a game with no colour barrier.

▶ A 1947 ad for a refrigerator.

▲ This is an upper middle-class house in the suburbs in 1948. People who lived in a house outside the city needed cars and lawnmowers. Most dads travelled quite a distance to their jobs. Most mothers did not work outside the home.

◀ Clothes in 1948 were simple. Women and young girls wore skirts and dresses. They rarely wore trousers. Children wore leather shoes every day. They brought soft-soled shoes to school for gym class.

Historical Map of America

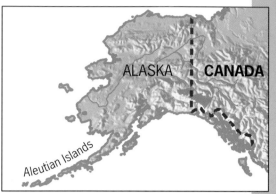

ALASKA **CANADA**

Aleutian Islands

On the map

By 1948, the United States included 48 states, the territories of Alaska and Hawaii, and the commonwealth of Puerto Rico. All parts of the United States suffered from the Great Depression of the 1930s and 1940s. The farms in the Dust Bowl were already suffering from the country's economic problems. However, America came out of World War II as one of the world's strongest countries. Most Americans once again had jobs and enough money to improve their lives. Millions moved out of cities into sprawling **suburbs**. Opportunities came last to minorities, especially African Americans.

Kauai

Oahu

Maui

Hawaii

HAWAIIAN ISLANDS

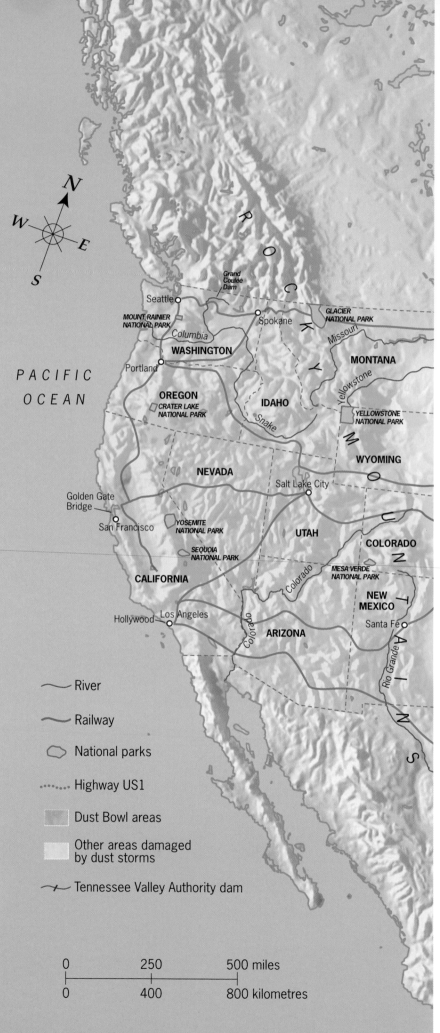

PACIFIC OCEAN

Seattle
Grand Coulée Dam
MOUNT RAINIER NATIONAL PARK
Columbia
Spokane
GLACIER NATIONAL PARK
Missouri
WASHINGTON
Portland
MONTANA
Yellowstone
OREGON
CRATER LAKE NATIONAL PARK
IDAHO
Snake
YELLOWSTONE NATIONAL PARK
WYOMING
NEVADA
Salt Lake City
Golden Gate Bridge
San Francisco
YOSEMITE NATIONAL PARK
UTAH
COLORADO
SEQUOIA NATIONAL PARK
Colorado
MESA VERDE NATIONAL PARK
CALIFORNIA
NEW MEXICO
Hollywood Los Angeles
Colorado
ARIZONA
Santa Fé
Rio Grande

R O C K Y   M O U N T A I N S

— River

— Railway

National parks

Highway US1

Dust Bowl areas

Other areas damaged by dust storms

Tennessee Valley Authority dam

0	250	500 miles
0	400	800 kilometres

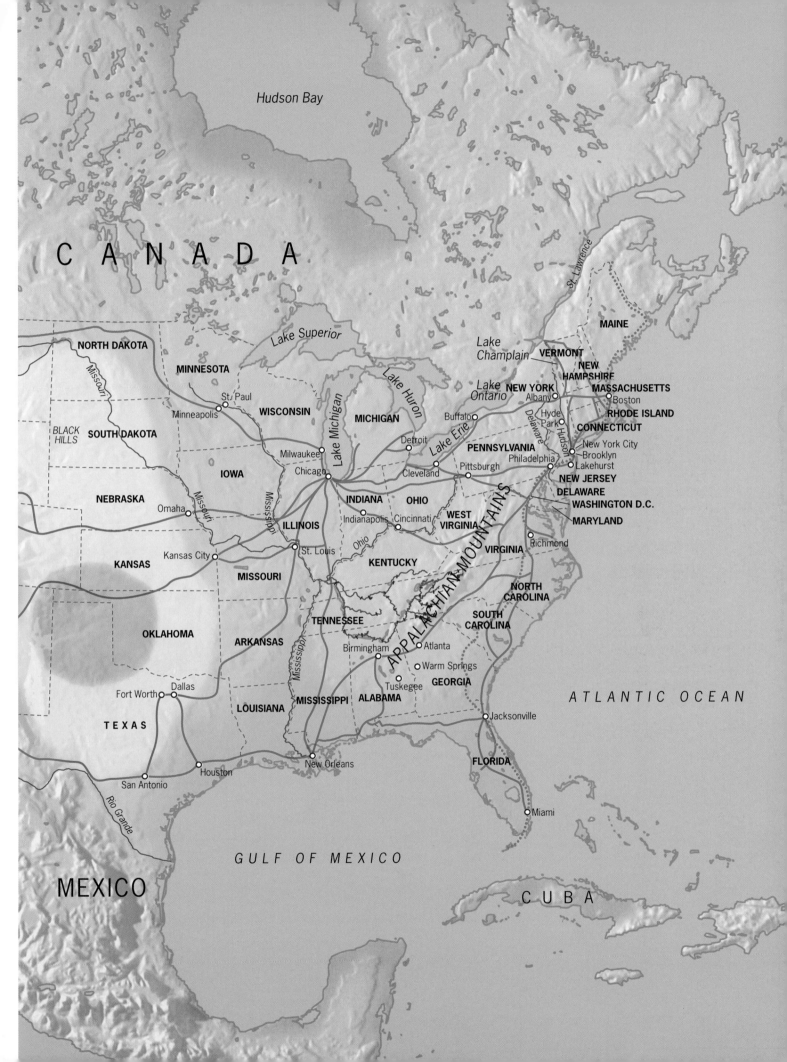

Hudson Bay

CANADA

NORTH DAKOTA

MINNESOTA

Lake Superior

St. Paul

Minneapolis

WISCONSIN

MICHIGAN

Lake Huron

MAINE

Lake Champlain

VERMONT

NEW HAMPSHIRE

Lake Ontario

NEW YORK

Albany

MASSACHUSETTS

Boston

BLACK HILLS

SOUTH DAKOTA

Buffalo

Hyde Park

RHODE ISLAND

CONNECTICUT

Milwaukee

IOWA

Chicago

Lake Michigan

Detroit

Lake Erie

PENNSYLVANIA

Cleveland

Pittsburgh

Philadelphia

Delaware

Hudson

New York City

Brooklyn

Lakehurst

Missouri

NEBRASKA

Omaha

Missouri

ILLINOIS

INDIANA

OHIO

NEW JERSEY

DELAWARE

WASHINGTON D.C.

MARYLAND

Indianapolis

Cincinnati

WEST VIRGINIA

Mississippi

St. Louis

Ohio

KANSAS

Kansas City

MISSOURI

KENTUCKY

VIRGINIA

Richmond

APPALACHIAN MOUNTAINS

NORTH CAROLINA

OKLAHOMA

ARKANSAS

TENNESSEE

SOUTH CAROLINA

Birmingham

Atlanta

Mississippi

Fort Worth

Dallas

Warm Springs

Tuskegee

GEORGIA

TEXAS

LOUISIANA

MISSISSIPPI

ALABAMA

ATLANTIC OCEAN

San Antonio

Houston

New Orleans

Jacksonville

FLORIDA

Rio Grande

St. Lawrence

GULF OF MEXICO

Miami

MEXICO

CUBA

FAMOUS PEOPLE OF THE TIME

Mary McLeod Bethune, 1875–1955, was a teacher who started a school for African American girls in 1904. FDR chose her as an advisor to head the National Youth Administration's Division of Negro Affairs. She was the first African American to head a government agency.

Winston Churchill, 1874–1965, was prime minister of Britain during World War II. His leadership and encouragement during the war years helped his country greatly. He met with FDR several times to discuss the goals of the war. In February 1945, he, FDR and Stalin signed an agreement that decided how Germany should be divided up after the war. This led to the Cold War.

Walt Disney, 1901–1966, was a cartoonist who created Mickey Mouse in 1928 and produced the first full-length animated cartoon in 1938: *Snow White and the Seven Dwarfs*. Later he created Disneyland in California and Disney World in Florida.

Albert Einstein, 1879–1955, was one of the greatest scientists of all time. He fled Nazi Germany because he was a Jew, and settled in the US. He met with FDR to explain how atomic energy could be used in the atomic bomb.

Dwight D. Eisenhower, 1890–1969, led the Allied troops in the invasion of Europe in 1944. After the war, he became Chief of Staff of the US Army. In 1953, he became the 34th US president. He was re-elected in 1957.

Adolf Hitler, 1889–1945, ruled Germany from 1933 until his death. He ordered the murder of millions of people as he tried to take over the world. His country lost World War II in 1945. He killed himself.

Herbert Hoover, 1874–1965, was US president when the Great Depression hit in 1929. At first he thought the nation could recover without government help. By 1932, he introduced some work programmes and relief money to the states. This was not enough to cure America's problems.

Douglas MacArthur, 1880–1964, was a five-star general of the US Army. He led the Allied army troops in the Pacific.

Benito Mussolini, 1883–1945, ruled Italy for 21 years, mostly as a dictator. He wanted to make Italy a powerful country but was unsuccessful. His country was defeated in World War II. His people executed him.

IMPORTANT DATES AND EVENTS

FRANKLIN D. ROOSEVELT
1882 born in Hyde Park, New York
1905 marries Eleanor Roosevelt
1911 elected state senator in New York
1913 appointed assistant Secretary of the Navy
1920 runs for US vice-president; does not win
1921 stricken with polio
1928 elected governor of New York
1932 elected president of the US
1933 Congress passes New Deal policies
1935 Social Security Act passes
1936 re-elected president
1939 agrees to sell arms to Allied countries
1940 re-elected president
1941 asks Congress to declare war on Japan after Pearl Harbour attack
1942 plans the beginning of the United Nations
1944 re-elected president
1945 dies on 12 April in Warm Springs, Georgia

OTHER EVENTS IN THE UNITED STATES 1929 to 1941
1929 stock market crashes; Great Depression begins
1930 population reaches 122 million; farmers in the mid-western Dust Bowl suffer from drought and winds
1931 'Star Spangled Banner' is adopted as America's official national anthem; Empire State Building opens; George Washington Bridge, linking Manhattan and New Jersey across the Hudson River, is completed
1932 Amelia Earhart becomes the first woman to fly solo across the Atlantic Ocean
1933 Congress starts the Tennessee Valley Authority; New Deal programmes begin; Prohibition ends
1934 Indian Reorganization Act attempts to protect Native American land and traditions
1936 Jesse Owens wins four gold metals at Berlin Olympics
1937 Golden Gate Bridge is completed; the *Hindenburg* crashes; pilot Amelia Earhart, attempting to fly around the world, disappears; Joe Louis becomes world heavyweight boxing champion
1938 Chester Carlson makes the first photocopy and calls it a 'xerox'
1940 America starts its first peacetime conscription of men into military service; population reaches 131.6 million
1941 US enters World War II; Great Depression ends as factories make war products

Jesse Owens, 1913–1981, was a record-breaking track athlete. He won four gold medals in the 1936 Olympics in Berlin. Germany's leader, Adolf Hitler, could not stand to see an African American win. He stormed out of the stadium. Owens accepted his medals.

George Patton Jr, 1885–1945, was an American general in the North African invasion and victory in France. He was quick to voice an opinion and was tough with the soldiers who served under him. His nickname was Old Blood and Guts.

Frances Perkins, 1882–1965, was Secretary for Labour [Work] under President Roosevelt. She was the first woman cabinet member.

Erwin Rommel, 1891–1944, was one of Germany's best military leaders during WWII. He led troops in North Africa and was eventually defeated by the British in 1942. His nickname was Desert Fox.

Eleanor Roosevelt, 1884–1962, was one of the most active first ladies in history. She travelled across the nation giving speeches and holding press conferences. She fought for equal rights for minority groups. From 1945 to 1951, she was a delegate to the United Nations General Assembly.

Franklin D. Roosevelt, 1882–1945, was the 32nd president of the US. He served 12 years. This was longer than any other president. He was elected to serve four more years, but died at the beginning of that term. Roosevelt led the US through the Great Depression and WWII.

Joseph Stalin, 1879–1953, was the head of the Soviet Union from 1924 to 1953. He was a dictator who killed or imprisoned people who threatened his power. During his leadership, the Soviet Union became a great world power.

John Steinbeck, 1902–1968, was a prize-winning author. He wrote about the struggles of poor people in such books as *The Grapes of Wrath* and *Tortilla Flat*.

Hideki Tojo, 1884–1948, was the Japanese leader who approved the attack on Pearl Harbour in 1941. He believed in fighting the war to its disastrous finish. When Japan lost the war, the Allies tried him as a war criminal and executed him.

Harry S. Truman, 1884–1972, was the 33rd US president. He was FDR's vice-president and took over the presidency when FDR died. Truman made one of the most powerful decisions of WWII – to drop the atomic bomb on Japan

---

US presidents from 1929 to 1948
Calvin Coolidge 1923–1929
Herbert C. Hoover 1929–1933
Franklin Delano Roosevelt 1933–1945
Harry S. Truman 1945–1953

OTHER EVENTS IN THE US 1942 to 1948
1942 Grand Coulee Dam is completed; Disney releases animated film *Bambi*
1945 America drops atomic bombs on two Japanese cities; World War II ends; the US joins the new United Nations, set up to keep world peace and security; New York becomes the world's financial capital, replacing London
1946 the world's first electronic computer is built
1947 Bernard Baruch coins the phrase 'Cold War' to describe non-military clashes between nations, especially the United States and the Soviet Union; African Americans are allowed to play baseball in the major leagues; pilot Chuck Yeager breaks the 'sound barrier', flying at a speed of 1,120 km/hr
1948 President Truman bans segregation in the armed forces; the US officially recognizes the State of Israel as an independent nation; baseball player Babe Ruth dies; Truman is re-elected

THE REST OF NORTH AND SOUTH AMERICA
1930 in Argentina, the military try to overthrow the government; in Brazil, Getúlio Vargas becomes president
1932–1935 war between Paraguay and Bolivia
1938 unsuccessful Nazi plots to overthrow the governments of Brazil and Chile
1941 Canada declares war on Japan
1942 Mexico and Brazil declare war on Germany and Japan
1943 a revolution in Argentina ends with Juan Peron becoming military dictator
1945 Vargas of Brazil overthrown by the military
1946 Peron becomes president of Argentina

THE REST OF THE WORLD
1930 British engineer Frank Whittle invents the jet engine
1931 Japanese invade China
1933 Nazis come to power in Germany
1934–1938 Stalin orders some 10 million people killed or sent to labour camps in the Soviet Union
1937 German engineer Wehrner von Braun builds the V2 rocket
1936 Spanish civil war begins
1939 World War II begins
1945 World War II ends; United Nations formed
1945–1946 Nuremberg Trials
1947 India and Pakistan gain independence from Britain
1948 Israel is created, and Burma and Ceylon (Sri Lanka) gain independence from Britain

GLOSSARY

Allied Powers (also called Allies) countries that fought Germany in World War I and World War II. They included the United States, Canada, Britain and France.

amendment changes in a document, such as the US Constitution

Atlantic Charter document that expressed the post-war goals of the United States and Britain, drawn up in August 1941

Axis Powers countries that fought the Allied Powers in World War II. They included Germany, Italy and Japan.

bomb shelter place to go for protection if an enemy attacks

bread line line of people waiting to get free food

capital city where the main offices of the government of a state or country are located

civil war war between people within a country

concentration camp prison camp for people thought to be dangerous to the government

Congress part of the US government that makes laws

dam barrier to hold back water

debt money or something else owing to someone

Depression a time in the 1930s when businesses in industrialized countries suffered and many people were unemployed

dictator ruler who has complete power, such as Adolf Hitler in Germany

election process of choosing someone by voting

gas chamber in concentration camps, a room where people stood while deadly gas filled the room

immigration movement of people who come to live in a country from other countries

inauguration ceremony to put someone in a position of leadership

insure agree to pay if something is lost

invade send armed forces into another country in order to take it over, as an invasion

liberation setting people free

Marines part of the US armed forces; marines are trained to fight on land and sea

military having to do with soldiers or war

mortgage loan from a bank to buy a house

mural painting on a wall

Nazi political group in Germany that restricted personal freedoms and used force to keep control

Negro term used to refer to people with dark skin, hair, and eyes; African American

New Deal name for programmes started by FDR to give people jobs and security

newsreel film about what is happening in the world that was shown at cinemas before the days of television

prime minister leader of a parliamentary government, such as Britain's

Prohibition period from 1920 to 1933 when it was illegal to make or sell alcoholic beverages

radiation long-lasting poison released from the atomic bomb

relief government programme that gives help to needy people

reservation area of land set aside by the government for a special purpose, such as a place for Native Americans to live

Secretary of the Navy the president's advisor in charge of the government's ships

senator person who is voted to be in the Senate, a part of government that makes laws

segregate to keep in a separate group, as in segregating African Americans from White people

soup kitchen place where volunteers cook meals for needy people

Soviet Union country that was once made up of 15 republics in eastern Europe and northern Asia. It included Russia.

statistician someone who keeps track of numbers during an event

stock market place where stocks and bonds are sold. If you own stock in a company, you have invested money in it.

suburb small community outside a large city

surrender to give up or admit that you cannot win

tax money that must be paid to a government which is used to run a town, state or country

union group of workers who join together to try to improve benefits, working conditions and wages

MORE BOOKS TO READ

The Grapes of Wrath, John Steinbeck

To Kill a Mocking Bird, Harper Lee, Heinemann, Oxford

Britain Since 1930, Stewart Ross, Evans Brothers Ltd, London 1999

The Great Depression, Stewart Ross, Evans Brothers Ltd, London 1999

Living Through History: Twentieth Century World, N. Kelly, R. Rees, J. Shuter, Heinemann, Oxford 1999

PLACES TO VISIT

The Imperial War Museum
Horseferry Road
London
SE1 6HZ
Telephone: 020 7416 5000

The American Museum in Britain
Claverton Manor
Bath BA2 7BD
Telephone: 01225 460 503

INDEX

INDEX